HORSES OF

BY DAHLOV IPCAR

LONG AGO

TIME CHART SHOWING STAGES IN THE
EVOLUTION OF THE HORSE

EPOCHS

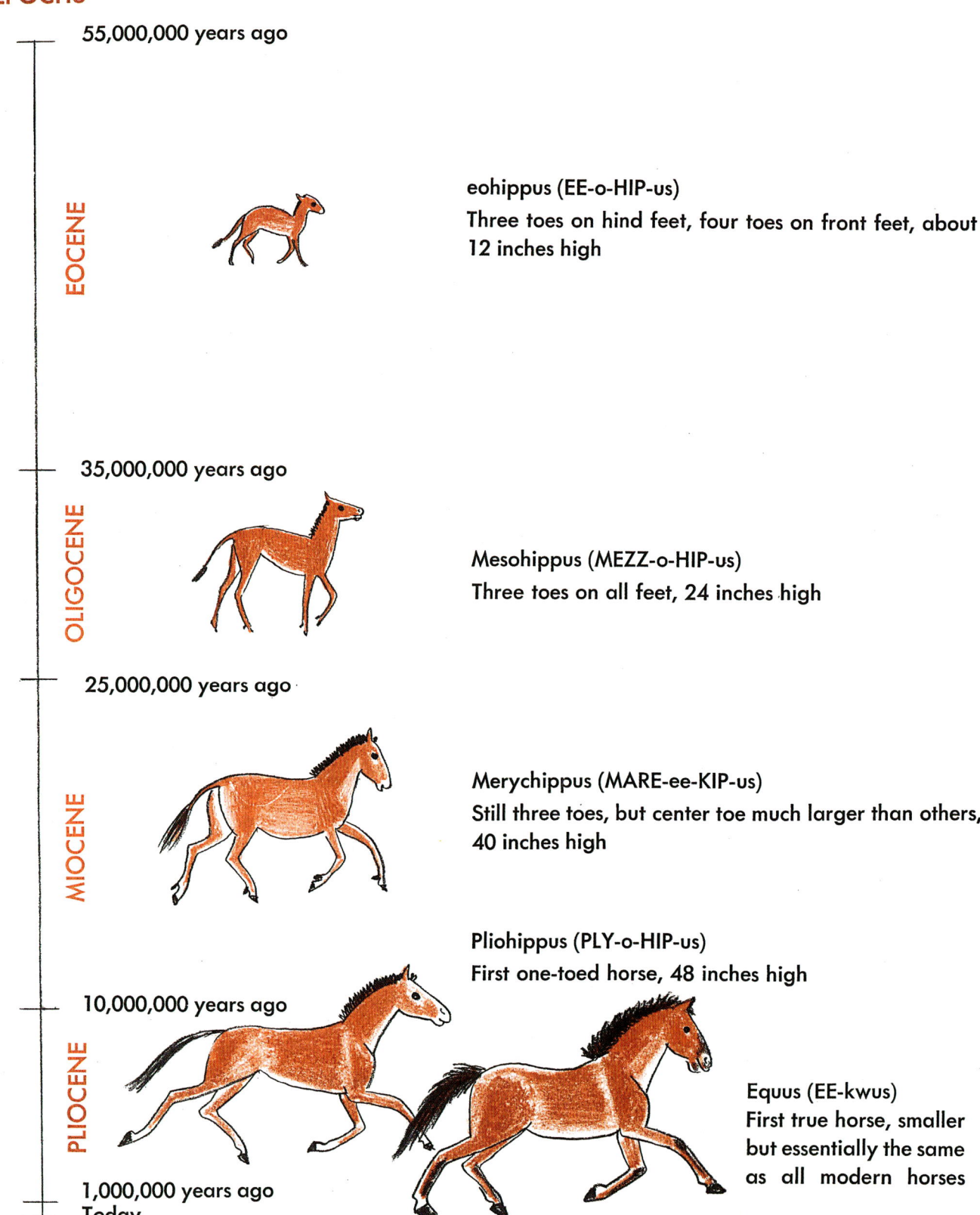

55,000,000 years ago

EOCENE

eohippus (EE-o-HIP-us)
Three toes on hind feet, four toes on front feet, about 12 inches high

35,000,000 years ago

OLIGOCENE

Mesohippus (MEZZ-o-HIP-us)
Three toes on all feet, 24 inches high

25,000,000 years ago

MIOCENE

Merychippus (MARE-ee-KIP-us)
Still three toes, but center toe much larger than others, 40 inches high

Pliohippus (PLY-o-HIP-us)
First one-toed horse, 48 inches high

10,000,000 years ago

PLIOCENE

1,000,000 years ago
Today

Equus (EE-kwus)
First true horse, smaller but essentially the same as all modern horses

One million years ago the Pleistocene Epoch began, and Equus came on the scene.
Twenty thousand years ago the Recent Epoch began, and men lived in caves.
Five thousand years ago the first civilizations in this book were just beginning.

THE FIRST HORSES

About fifty million years ago, eohippus, a little animal the size of a fox, lived in the green, leafy woods of North America. He had four toes on his front feet and three toes on his hind feet, and a very small brain.

After forty million years of slow changes, eohippus finally evolved into a horse. His descendant Pliohippus ended up running on only one toe, or hoof, and he was much larger and smarter than eohippus had been.

The first true horse, Equus, looked like a stocky pony with a short stiff mane. These early horses ran wild over much of the world and formed large herds wherever there was open grassland But they all died out in America long before the white man came. In Europe these original wild horses were called "tarpans." Tarpans were hunted for their meat for thousands of years; until finally in the nineteenth century, they, too, were all killed off.

However, even today a few of the early horses, or ones very much like them, are still running wild in Mongolia. Now they are called "Przewalski" horses (pronounced Persia-VAL-skee). They are the only true wild horses left from prehistoric times.

Twenty thousand years ago Cro-Magnon cave men hunted the tarpans and painted pictures of them on the walls of their caves.

At this time the only domestic animal was the dog.

Sumerian chariot pulled by four onagers

THE HORSE IS TAMED (about 2500 B.C.)

When men first became farmers rather than hunters, they domesticated cattle, sheep, goats, pigs, and donkeys. All these animals had been domesticated by 4000 B.C. But the horse was not tamed until at least a thousand years later. Probably the early horses were almost untamable, like the zebras of Africa. Zebras, although members of the horse family, have never been domesticated.

No one knows who first managed to catch and train the wild horses. Probably the first real horsemen were nomadic tribes living on the plains where large herds of wild horses grazed. Herders of cattle and sheep would naturally become herders and riders of horses.

But strange to say, when the horse first appears in history he was hitched to a chariot rather than ridden horseback. There were many kingdoms and many wars in the ancient world. One of the first and most important uses for horses was to pull war chariots.

As long ago as 3500 B.C. the Sumerians in Mesopotamia drove war chariots —even before they had horses. Their chariots were pulled by "onagers" (large Asiatic asses, now wild). Horses were first brought into this region by warrior tribes from Western Asia—the Kassites, Hittites, and Hyksos—who invaded the Middle East with their chariots about 1750 B.C. The Hyksos succeeded in conquering the rich land of Egypt.

The Egyptians finally drove the invaders out, but from them they learned the use of the horse and chariot. And then the Egyptians went on to build up vast armies, using chariots, to conquer a great empire of their own.

The early horses brought into Egypt resembled the Przewalski horse, but later the Egyptians obtained from Africa a far superior breed of horse, taller and more elegantly shaped, and with finer bone structure. These horses were used to improve the Egyptian stock and were also introduced into Arabia. The ancient horse of Africa is believed to be the foundation stock from which the remarkable Arabian horses later developed.

Wherever there are horses there are horse traders. The Phoenicians were the chief seafarers and traders of the ancient world. They traded the different breeds of horses throughout all the countries of the Mediterranean, even far into the wilds of Northern Europe and the British Isles, and also sold chariots for the horses to pull.

Phoenician ship loading horses

Egyptian chariots in battle.

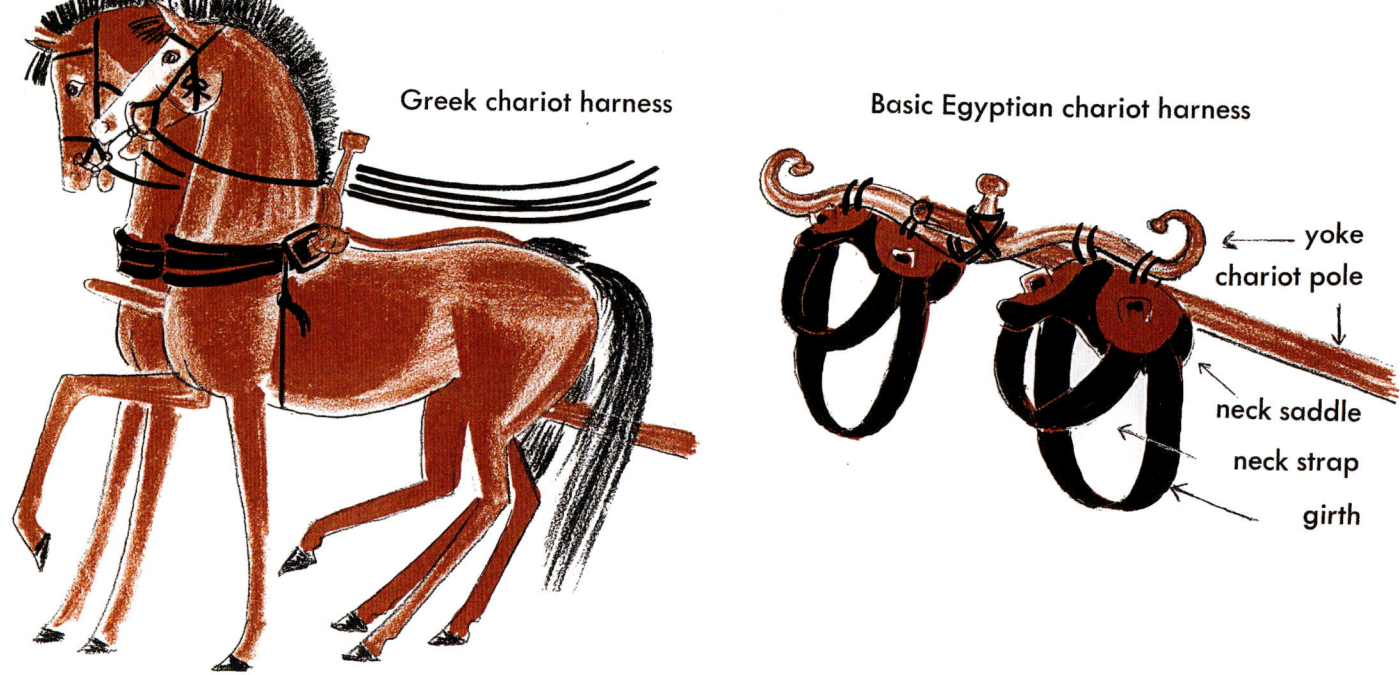

Greek chariot harness

Basic Egyptian chariot harness

← yoke
chariot pole
↓

neck saddle

neck strap

girth

CHARIOTS AND HARNESS

Usually a chariot carried a driver and a bowman or spearman; it made a moving platform from which to attack the enemy. Chariots were devastating to the foot soldiers—they were the equivalent of tanks in modern warfare.

The chariot was pulled by a pole fastened to a light yoke that fitted across the back of the horse's neck and was held in place by a wide neck strap. But harnessed in this way, a horse could not pull a very heavy load; and often three or four horses were hitched to one light chariot.

Oxen work well under the yoke because they have powerful neck muscles. But the horse is built differently—a horse's pulling power is in his shoulders. With only a strap around his neck, the horse could not pull his full strength into the job.

It was a poor way to hitch up a horse, but for over three thousand years this was the only type of harness men knew. This is one of the main reasons why

Some examples of early bridles and bits

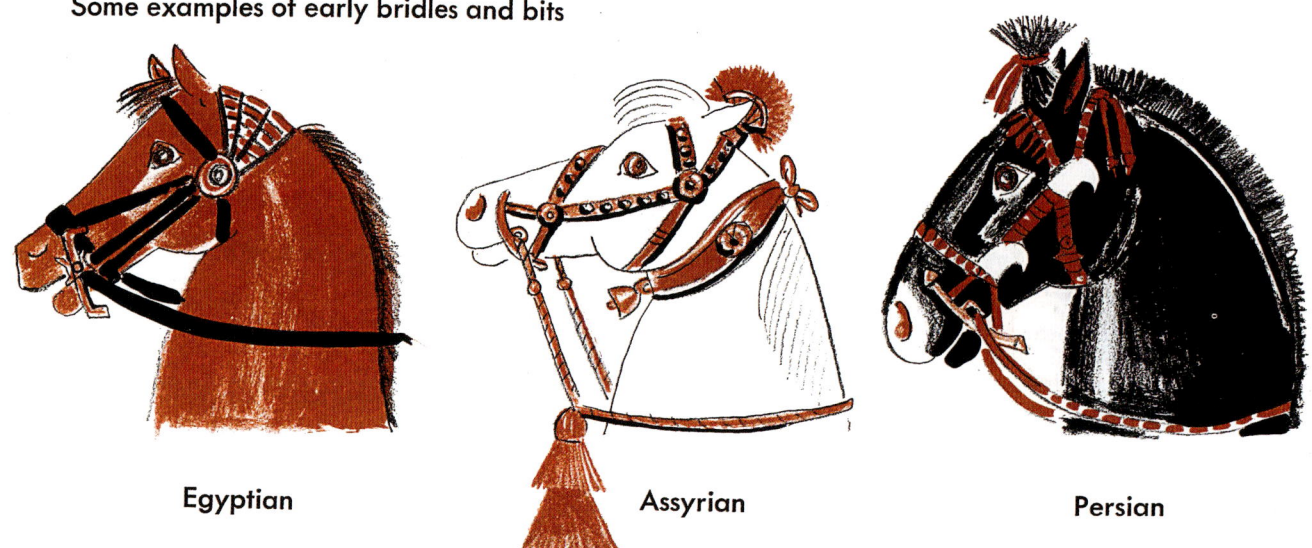

Egyptian   Assyrian   Persian

Yoke of oxen pulling plow

horses were seldom used as work animals in ancient times. It would have taken a large number of horses to pull a real load, and horses were much too valuable to be wasted this way when oxen were cheaper and could do the work easier. So the horse was used only as a war machine. Oxen did the heavy work such as plowing, and donkeys did the light work such as carrying packs.

To most of these early people the horse was a new and terrifying animal; they did not dare risk getting on its back. Although the Egyptians drove horses in chariots they never did much riding and never learned to fight from horseback.

The Assyrians were the first of the Near Eastern people to learn to ride well. By 700 B.C. they had large numbers of mounted warriors—or cavalry—in their army. They had no saddles, but used saddle cloths. Bridles and bits were basically the same as modern ones; but the lack of a saddle with stirrups made fighting from horseback difficult for the next thousand years.

Scythian   Greek   Roman

Lion hunting was a favorite sport of Assyrian kings and nobles.

PERSIANS AND SCYTHIANS (550–331 B.C.)

The Persians, who followed the Assyrians, also used much cavalry. In battle the Persian archers kept up a hail of arrows while the cavalry rode around the fringes of the fight throwing the enemy lines into confusion and pursuing them vigorously if they fled. The Persians also developed a type of chariot with long curved blades attached to the wheels that could mow down everything in its path.

They conquered a vast empire in the Middle East, all the way from Greece to India. From India the Persians brought war elephants to use in battle. Untrained horses would not face elephants. The sight or smell of these strange beasts threw the horses into panic, and most cavalry was completely useless against them.

The Persians built good roads and established a royal mail service, using fast mounted riders in relays like our pony express. A journey of 1500 miles that usually took three months was covered by the royal post in seven to fourteen days.

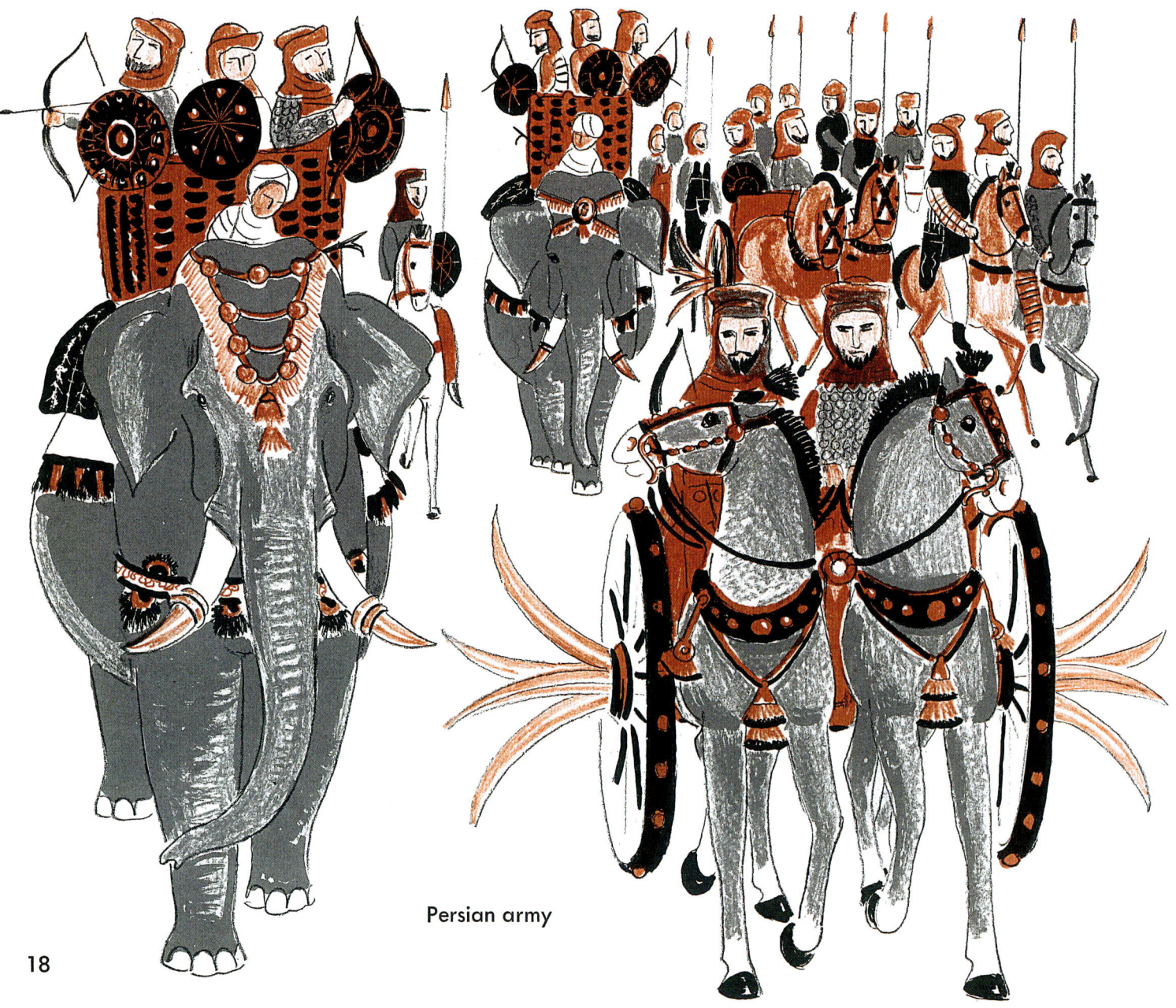

Persian army

18

The royal mail

But there were some people the Persians could not conquer. All along the northern borders of the empire lived the Scythians who kept up a steady harassment of Persian settlements.

The Scythians were the most expert horsemen of ancient times. Their culture was based on horses. They were nomads with huge herds of horses and cattle, and they lived on horse meat and mare's milk. They roamed freely over the vast plains of southern Russia and Siberia and even into far Mongolia.

The Scythians were rich in metals, especially gold. Their clothing and the harnesses of their horses were often decorated with solid gold. Some Scythians had saddles—but without stirrups.

Their kings were given lavish burials, usually the king's wives and personal attendants would be buried with him. This was considered a great honor, as they believe they would go on serving their king in the next world. The king's favorite horses were also slaughtered and buried with him. As many as 360 horses have been found in one burial mound. A year after the king's death, fifty young men and fifty horses were killed and stuffed and mounted around his tomb to guard it.

When the Persian armies attacked them, the Scythian horsemen would not stand and fight. They galloped away out of sight and waited until the enemy was strung out on the march; then they attacked swiftly and fiercely, and as swiftly withdrew again. Like the American Indians they took the scalps of their enemies. These they hung on the reins of their horses. Also they burned the pastures and filled in the wells, until the Persians were forced to retreat, usually with heavy losses.

Scythians were always on the move. The women did not ride horseback but travelled in "homes on wheels"—large carts covered with black felt canopies, pulled by large teams of horses or oxen.

Because they had so many horses, the Scythians could be extravagant in the size of their teams!

Boar hunt

THE GREEKS (800–300 B.C.)

Horses were never plentiful in Greece and were owned only by the rich. But the Greek upper classes loved all sports that required courage and skill, and they became expert horsemen, doing much racing and hunting. Greeks admired horses above all animals; their artists produced some of the handsomest horse painting and sculpture of all time.

Greece was not a unified country. It was made up of many small city states that were always fighting among themselves. The early Greeks drove chariots into battle, but did little fighting with them; and as Greece was a mountainous land with few roads, chariots fell into disuse. For many centuries they were not used in war—only for parades and races—and all fighting was done on foot.

When the Greeks were attacked by the Persians in the fifth century B.C. they

Racing chariots 500 B.C.

managed to defeat the invaders. But they saw how effective the Persian cavalry was for scouting and swift attacks, and they soon developed their own.

The Greek cavalry made a colorful show, but they were not very useful on the battlefield until taken in hand by Philip of Macedon, who united the Greeks in a league against Persia in 337 B.C.

He divided the cavalry into three parts: "heavy horse," well-armored for charging into battle; "light horse" for scouting; and "'dragoons" who fought on horseback or on foot as needed. He trained the cavalry to work with the infantry, and under Philip's generalship they became a really first-class fighting force.

In fact they became so effective that under his son, Alexander the Great, the Greeks managed to bring about the complete downfall of the mighty Persian Empire in 331 B.C.

The Greek cavalry was made up of young noblemen who used their own horses. All Greeks provided their own battle equipment. There was no uniform, but the cavalry wore the same sort of bronze armor as the foot soldiers.

It was difficult for an armored man to mount a horse without stirrups. Some cavalrymen trained their horses to kneel, and others used their spears to pole vault onto the horses' backs.

Heavy cavalry
second century A.D.

THE ROMANS (200 B.C.–A.D. 300)

The early Romans were often defeated in battle due to their lack of cavalry. As in most ancient wars, it was the use of the horse that made the difference between success and failure. When a cavalry force was raised by the Roman general Scipio in 200 B.C. the Romans went on to many victories and built a great empire.

However, for a long time the Romans depended more on foot soldiers than cavalry. In the beginning a standard Roman legion was made up of 3000 infantry and 300 horses. But by A.D. 250 the cavalry had become so important that one third of the army was on horseback.

The Roman cavalry, like the Greek, was made up of young men able to provide their own horses. They were given the title af "equite," and they formed an important class in Roman society.

In Roman times the first horseshoes came into use. Before this cavalry had been much troubled by their horses' hoofs wearing down under hard use. Some horsemen had tried using leather socks or straw sandals on their horses' feet, but these had to be replaced too often. Now for the first time, iron plates were nailed directly to the hoof. They did not hurt the horse and proved very long-wearing. After this all horses that did hard work were fitted with iron horseshoes.

When the Romans conquered Europe they found different kinds of horses being used in different countries. In Flanders they found large heavy-boned horses with feathery fetlocks. This Flemish stock helped improve the size of the Roman horses.

In Britain they found tough little horses pulling crude chariots. These British chariots were used mainly to bring soldiers up to the battle lines. The British believed that a man draws strength from the soil he stands on, so they fought on foot. This belief kept them from learning to ride for almost six hundred years after the Romans came.

The Romans did not use chariots in war. But they developed many different types of wagons and carts for different uses, including four-wheeled covered wagons. All Romans loved pageantry and every victory was celebrated with a triumphant parade. Ornate and heavy parade chariots were used for these processions, often pulled by teams of ten or more horses.

Triumphal chariot
second century A.D.

27

The Romans, like the Greeks, enjoyed chariot races, and charioteers were popular heroes. The usual race was seven times around the course.

Race tracks were called "circuses." At the Circus Maximus in Rome 250,000 people could watch the races.

THE FALL OF ROME AND AFTER (A.D. 350–1000)

The Roman Empire lasted five hundred years, but in the end it was destroyed by fierce mounted Germanic tribes who poured down from the wilds of Northern Europe, and by the Huns who invaded from the east. The Huns were especially skilled horsemen, a nomadic people who had been living and fighting on horseback for hundred of years.

Although the Romans had increased their cavalry, they made the mistake of using the horse troops as frontier guards only. On frontier duty they were far from home, their morale was low, and they fought poorly.

Saddles with stirrups had been used in Asia for some time. It was during this period that they reached Europe, and the Visigoths learned to use them. With this new device they outrode the Roman horsemen; and , to the surprise of the Romans, beat them soundly, almost annihilating three Roman legions in one big battle in A.D. 378.

The Roman government called back troops from all its outposts in Britain and Europe, but they could not save Rome. Roman rule was overthrown, law and government vanished, and confusion reigned in Europe for many centuries.

Visigoths looting a village

Bands of mounted warriors roamed the countryside, looting and fighting. Each warrior chieftain had to protect himself and his men as best he could. They soon built themselves small forts, and each tried to defend some piece of land with his own small army. This was the start of the feudal system. The small forts became big castles. The chieftains became great lords or kings with many armed men under them. War was the main business of all the upper classes, and they all rode horses. The horse made the man who rode him important—something above the common man.

Saddles were in general use, and stirrups now made it possible for an armored man to mount and dismount easily. Knights could wear more and more armor. In the beginning chain mail was the most popular kind.

Against armored knights the ordinary foot soldier of the time was almost helpless as he was very poorly armed (with whatever weapons he could find for himself). The infantry ceased to be a body of trained soldiers and became just a rabble of peasantry. In fact, the man on foot was considered of so little importance that in battle he was often trampled underfoot and injured more by the knights of his own side than by the enemy.

Eleventh century knights in battle.

CRUSADERS AND SARACENS (A.D. 1096–1291)

In the twelveth and thirteenth centuries the knights of Christian Europe were inspired to go on a series of "Crusades" to free the Holy Land of Palestine from the Moslems who had conquered all of the Near East, North Africa, and Spain.

The Crusaders brought their heavy war horses across the Mediterranean Sea, and there they met the Saracens—Arabians, who were mounted on light, swift horses. The Saracens wore flowing robes, no armor, and carried light weapons. They were desert fighters who did not attack head on but rode in rings around the big, lumbering horses of the Crusaders and inflicted terrible damage with a series of swift attacks and retreats.

The damage was mostly to the horses, as the knights were well protected with armor. But when their horses were shot out from under them the knights had to fight on foot which they considered an indignity. They finally began to cover their horses with chain mail from head to tail to protect them from arrows. Over the mail they put a cloth drapery to keep the iron from rusting.

The Arabian horses were the best in the world, for the Arabs had been carefully breeding them for centuries, always striving to improve them. They mem-

orized the lineage of each horse, passing it on by word of mouth, often using very flowery language. The best horses were idolized like famous people, and sometimes an enemy's life would be spared just because of the horse he rode.

Arabian horses were very gentle. They lived with the family and were treated like pets. They were never ridden until fully grown, but then they were given a very severe endurance test—for endurance was the quality most highly prized by the Arabs. Only mares were tested, as they were considered most important. Each young mare was ridden at top speed for over fifty miles, then made to plunge into deep water and swim some distance. If she showed signs of exhaustion, she was rejected as unfit to maintain the best bloodlines.

The Crusaders never succeeded in freeing the Holy Land; and after many long, exhausting campaigns they finally gave up and went home to take care of their own lands, which were often badly neglected during their long absences.

The Crusaders took home many Arab horses. But the Arabian horses were small, and large horses were needed to carry armored knights; so the Arabian stock was not kept pure, but was mixed with the heavy breeds. Arab blood added many superior qualities of bone, wind, endurance, and beauty.

Like all horsemen the Arabs were always eager to race. The desert tribesmen prided themselves on being tough warriors and scorned fancy trappings and other finery.

CHINESE AND MONGOLS (A.D. 1200–1300)

Most horses of ancient China were of the "Bactrian" type: heavy-bodied, deep-chested, with well-arched necks. They were used to pull high-wheeled carriages and ridden by both men and women.

China was a rich land of fertile plains bordered on the north by the vast barren wastelands of Mongolia, where tribes of fierce warlike horsemen roamed. Horses were plentiful in China because of the nearby Mongolian horse herds.

The Mongols—like the Scythians and Huns—lived almost entirely on horseback. The horse was the most important thing in their lives. They caught horses from their herds by fishing for them with a noose on the end of a long flexible pole. One very fast "lasso horse" was always kept tied close to camp to be used in catching others. Life on the Mongolian plains was very hard, especially when drought ruined the pasturage, and the rich lands of China were often a temptation to these poorer neighbors.

China was raided so often by Mongol warriors that finally in 228 B.C. the Emperor Ch'in Shih Huang Ti built a massive wall, twenty feet high and 1400 miles long, to keep out these "barbarians." But the "Great Wall" failed to protect China from the Mongols.

For a brief time during the thirteenth century the Mongols rose suddenly to world power under the leadership of Genghis Khan. He was a genius in the use of cavalry and vanquished every country that he invaded, including Russia and Hungary. His army was made up entirely of horsemen with no foot soldiers.

Genghis Khan invaded China by bribing his way through a pass in the Great Wall and eventually conquered all of that huge country. The Mongols were the last of the invading hordes of nomadic horsemen who had so often swept down from the plains to attack and destroy the great civilizations of the world.

The Mongols ruled China for the next hundred years, but the Chinese managed to absorb their conquerors and preserve their own civilization. The Chinese were an inventive and artistic people. They invented silk and gunpowder and fine porcelain. The Chinese probably also deserve credit for inventing the saddle and stirrups, at least saddles with stirrups appear in Chinese tomb art long before such devices were known in Europe.

Instead of burying real horses in their graves the Chinese made charming statuettes of horses and other animals which they placed in the "spirit chamber" of tombs to serve their dead masters in the afterlife.

A Chinese family starting on a journey.

THE JAPANESE (A.D. 1200–1300)

The horse seems to have been the first domestic animal known in Japan. The Japanese came originally from Asia and brought their horses with them. They invaded and settled the islands sometime before A.D. 400.

Japanese horses were quite small, many were pony-size; but they were stocky and strong enough to carry armored men on their backs. The horse was highly respected and always well cared for in Japan. Horses were never driven in harness; the high, covered, two-wheel carts that carried women and wealthy citizens were pulled by single oxen.

The Japanese adopted most of their culture from the Chinese, but from the beginning they were a warlike nation. Different clans were always fighting with each other. There was always a large cavalry force: a division was made up of 600 horse and 400 foot soldiers. Ambushes and surprise raids were common, but the Japanese most enjoyed the formal battle. Each clan carried flags into battle and it was a colorful and ceremonious affair.

Their main weapon was the long bow—up to seven and a half feet long— and their swords were long too. The warriors were called "samurai," and they were very proud of their profession. They underwent severe training in all the arts of war, especially horsemanship.

They wore plate armor of iron and leather which hung loosely. Their horses had colorful trappings and elegantly ornamented saddles, often beautifully inlaid with gold and silver. The stirrups looked like "scuff" slippers, but served their purpose. Later, horses were protected with chain mail and wore weird iron masks with demon faces on their heads. It is a wonder that these small horses could carry all this weight.

INDIA (up to A.D. 1600)

In India a rich culture developed about 2500 B.C. in the Indus River valley. Humped cattle, water buffalo, and camels were domesticated—and perhaps elephants. The horse was brought into India by Aryan invaders from the northwest who conquered the original inhabitants and took over the country about 1500 B.C.

These invaders were a warrior race who rode horses and drove chariots. At this time the elephant was not used in war, but later elephants and horses were both used.

The Aryans had large herds of cattle, and horses were never as important to them as cows. Originally they were beef eaters, but later the Hindu religion made many animals sacred, especially cows. Under this religious law, cattle could no longer be butchered or eaten, and they kept multiplying until eventually there seemed to be as many cows as people in India.

Horses are less hardy than cattle. They cannot stand heat and drought and the frequent famines that occur in India; so even though horses too were highly esteemed they never overran the country like the cows. Horses were bred chiefly in the northwest and in Sind where the climate was cooler. They were owned mainly by the warrior classes, and by kings and princes who kept large stables of fine horses. The parade trappings of the royal horses were extremely elaborate, embellished with gold and jewels and embroidery, and hung with numerous bells and tassels.

In the sixteenth century A.D. the Moguls from Persia became the rulers of India, and there was much exchange of culture between the courts of India and Persia. For the next three centuries artists traveled between both countries and painted many beautiful miniatures of Indian and Persian horses to illustrate books for the royal libraries. One of their favorite subjects was the game of polo which the Persians introduced into India at this time.

Great Horse and knight in fifteenth-century plate armor

EUROPE IN THE LATER MIDDLE AGES (A.D. 1300–1500)

In Europe during the thirteenth or fourteenth century the horse collar was invented. Like saddles and horseshoes this was an important change. It was a great improvement over the old yoke and neck strap. Now for the first time horses could pull heavy loads efficiently. But the best and strongest horses were still used in war, and only the old or broken-down ones were used as work horses.

In these same centuries better bows and arrows were developed. Longbows and crossbows came into use. They were very powerful and could shoot an arrow through ordinary chain mail and even light plate armor. Now the infantry came back into its own, and for a while archers on foot were as important as the knights.

Knights wore heavier and heavier armor, complete suits made of fitted plates of steel; and they armored their horses too. The best armor was tested for strength by shooting at it with a crossbow.

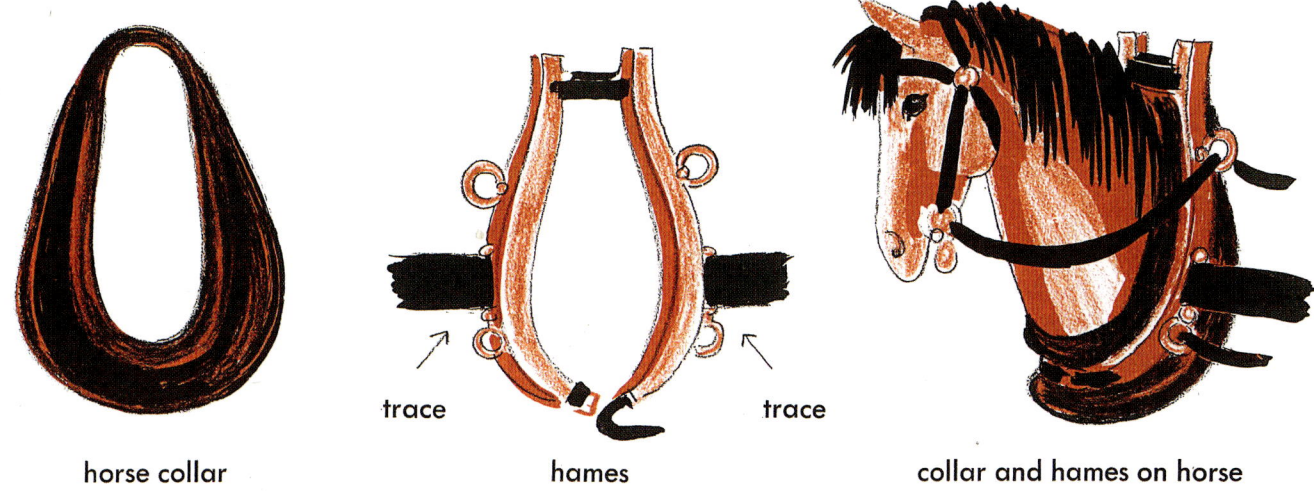

horse collar   trace   hames   trace   collar and hames on horse

The traces that do the pulling are fastened to the hames.

The use of stirrups also made it possible to use longer, heavier lances. The butt rested on the stirrup when not in use. Before long, knights were carrying lances up to fourteen feet long, which was the longest length that could be handled on horseback.

It took a very strong horse to carry a fully armored knight, who might weigh 400 pounds or more. Heavy horses had to be developed, and the ancient horse of Flanders was used to build up a new breed called "Great Horses", capable of carrying all this weight.

A great deal of ceremony grew up around the knights. They held tournaments that had started as war games but finally became enormous, fantastic pageants. Each knight had his colors and his device painted on his shield and on his horse's drapery. Crests on helmets became wildly fanciful, and horses also wore crests on their heads to match those of their riders.

There were many kinds of mock combat at tournaments, but the favorite was "jousting."

In the joust two knights charged
each other with lances, each trying to unhorse the other.

Seventeenth-century cavaliers. Their horses are still of fairly heavy build.

GUNS COME INTO USE (A.D. 1500–1700)

In the fourteenth century the first cannons and guns had been invented, but it took almost two hundred years before they were perfected and became really useful weapons.

The first guns were very weak, and the balls they shot could do little more than put a dent in armor plate. But by the end of the sixteenth century, guns were so powerful that bullets could pierce even the heaviest armor.

Heavier and heavier armor was made, finally it became so heavy that once a knight had tumbled from his horse he was completely helpless. He could not even get back on his feet. And in order to mount he had to be hoisted onto his horse's back with a block and tackle. But even this armor did not stop bullets.

Armor could not be made any heavier, so for all practical purposes it became useless. But the knights hated to give it up; they still kept it around for parades and tournaments. On the battlefield they used only lightweight half-armor, or just a breastplate and helmet.

The heavy horses were no longer needed; now the nobles preferred light, swift horses. The knight became a "cavalier"—that is: a gentleman soldier—armed with a musket or pistols, and instead of a lance and heavy broadsword he carried

Cavalier's "lackeys" who carry extra pistols and ammunition for their masters.

a light, thin rapier.

In the seventeenth century Arabian horses were again imported into Europe and England, and Arab blood went into producing the elegant type of horse the cavaliers desired.

Horse races had been held since horses were first ridden, but organized race meets of the kind known today started in the sixteenth century. This was when horse racing became "the sport of kings." Racing was encouraged by the interest of royalty in fast, light horses, and it has flourished ever since.

All the armies of Europe now had large numbers of heavy horses on hand— and no use for them; so they were put to work on farms or pulling freight wagons. For the first time real horsepower was plentiful for farmers; and because of this sudden supply of heavy draft horses, farmers began to try new farming methods.

The surplus of horses also resulted in the establishment of stagecoach routes which now sprang up between cities. Inns along the highways became relay stations supplying fresh horses to the stage lines, and travel became faster and easier.

Seventeenth-century stagecoach changing horses at a country inn. The coachman carries a blunderbuss as protection against highwaymen.

SPANIARDS AND INDIANS (A.D. 1500–1800)

In searching for a new sea route to India, Columbus had discovered America. The Spanish, in the sixteenth century, were busy exploring and conquering this New World.

They still found armor useful at this time, for the combination of the new firearms and the old heavy armor won them many victories. They brought their war horses and cannon with them across the sea, and with these they conquered the great Inca and Aztec civilizations of Peru and Mexico. Their horses and guns terrified the Indians, and their armor protected the Spanish "conquistadors" from the spears, and arrows and axes which were the only weapons the Indians had.

The Indians had no domestic animals except llamas and dogs and guinea pigs; but they still remembered ancient traditions about the horse. They told the Spaniards that long ago their ancestors had tried to keep horses, but that they had all died of a sickness caused by the bites of vampire bats.

When the Spanish explored North America some of their horses were left behind to run free in Texas. These were later joined by horses that escaped from the great ranches established by the Spaniards in Mexico. Whatever disease had killed off the original wild horses of America must have died with them, for the Spanish horses flourished in the wilderness. Within two hundred years they had multiplied into large herds of "mustangs" (from the Spanish word mesteño, meaning strayed or wild). With the buffalo and antelope they roamed the Great Plains that run through the central United States from Texas into Canada.

The coming of the horse changed the lives of the plains Indians completely. Within a few generations they had learned to use the horse and become expert riders. Before this they had traveled on foot with only dogs to help drag their belongings. Now they used horses and followed the buffalo herds.

When the American pioneers began to settle the West, they had a hard time with these Indian warriors who were highly skilled at fighting on horseback.

Plains Indians hunting buffalo.

Eighteenth-century dray horses

THE HORSE AT WORK (A.D. 1700–1900)

Meanwhile in Europe, with the use of draft horses, farming methods began rapidly to improve. Now farm machinery was invented: seed drills, cultivators, mowers, rakes, and reapers—all for horses to pull. However, oxen still did most of the farm work until the end of the eighteenth century, because many farmers were slow to change their ways. But they began to find the horse more useful; the same horse could mow the fields, haul in the crops, and carry the farmer to town on his back. And only horses were both fast enough and strong enough to pull the new machines.

In the eighteenth and nineteenth centuries horses did almost everything. Besides being used for coaches and farm work and sports, they pulled barges, trains, wagons, and fire engines.

In England during this period much attention was paid to horse breeding.

Steeplechase 1830

Five horse team pulling McCormick reaper 1870

Draft horses were bred that were even larger and stronger than the Great Horses that carried the knights. Special horses were bred for special purposes: medium-weight horses for coaches and carriages, sturdy light jumpers for hunting, easy-gaited horses for riding, small ponies for work in the mines. But probably most attention was paid to the breeding of race horses. All the Thoroughbreds of today trace back to three famous Arab stallions imported in the late seventeenth and early eighteenth centuries.

In the 1600's and later the colonists brought many horses with them when they settled America; and since there were very few roads, the horse was the main means of travel. Heavy horses were especially bred in Pennsylvania where the big covered Conestoga wagons were built. These wagons could carry freight over rough country, and even float across rivers.

When cattlemen moved into the Great Plains, the cowboys lassoed and broke the wild mustangs for use on the big cattle ranches. Later the plains were settled and broken up into farms. The huge size of the new Western farms encouraged farmers to buy bigger and better farm machines.

As the use of machinery spread on the farms, one invention led to another. Steam engines were invented for hauling passenger and freight trains, and used on farms for heavy tractors and threshing machines. Finally at the end of the nineteenth century the gasoline engine was invented. Then trucks and cars and tractors took over most of the work of the horse. And now once again the horse is used as he was in early times: for riding, sports, and for herding cattle.

All through the long centuries horses have changed men's lives. And even though machines have taken their places, horses will probably still be with us for a long time, if only for the pleasure they give us.

A NOTE ABOUT THE PICTURES

The pictures in this book are all based on the actual art of ancient times. However, I have used this material freely; nothing is copied directly except some details of equipment and costume.

I have drawn my galloping horses as ancient artists did rather than in the photographic gallop that we are now used to. I feel the artists of the past came much nearer to capturing the horse's true motion than the camera does. The grotesque and ungainly positions into which the camera freezes the gallop convey none of the feeling of swift and flowing movement that we see when we watch a living horse in action.

Famous race in 1830 between the first U.S. built steam locomotive, *Tom Thumb,* and a horse-drawn train. The horse won because *Tom Thumb* broke down, but this was the last victory for the horse.

ABOUT THE AUTHOR

Dahlov Ipcar, who lives on Robinhood Farm near Bath, Maine, writes and paints when she isn't busy helping her husband and sons with the farm work. Mrs. Ipcar has been painting ever since she can remember and has had many one-man shows in Maine and in New York City, where one of her canvases hangs in the permanent collection of the Metropolitan Museum of Art. She is the author and illustrator of many picture books.

Down East Books

Published by Down East Books
A wholly owned subsidiary of The Rowman & Littlefield Publishing Group, Inc.
4501 Forbes Boulevard, Suite 200, Lanham, Maryland 20706
www.rowman.com

16 Carlisle Street, London W1D 3BT, United Kingdom

Distributed by NATIONAL BOOK NETWORK

Originally published in 1965 by Doubleday and Company, Inc.

British Library Cataloguing in Publication Information Available

Library of Congress Cataloging-in-Publication Data

Library of Congress Control Number: 2014936651

ISBN 978-1-60893-323-5 (cloth : alk. paper) — ISBN 978-1-60893-325-9 (electronic)

∞™ The paper used in this publication meets the minimum requirements of
American National Standard for Information Sciences—Permanence of Paper
for Printed Library Materials, ANSI/NISO Z39.48-1992.

Printed in Malaysia